Englanninkielisen populaarimusiikin
parhaat bändit ja piisit

MATTI RANTA

Englanninkielisen populaarimusiikin parhaat bändit ja piisit

© 2016 Matti Ranta
Päällys ja taitto: Books on Demand
Kustantaja: BoD – Books on Demand, Helsinki, Suomi
Valmistaja: BoD – Books on Demand, Norderstedt, Saksa
ISBN: 978-952-330-827-5

SISÄLTÖ

KIITOKSET

Kirjan tekeminen on ollut täysin riippuvainen Internetin tiedoista. Toiseksi paljon apua on ollut Billboard musiikkilehden tiedoista, jotka nekin löytyvät Internetistä. Kun henkilö etsii kaikkia parhaita musiikkikappaleita, mitä on olemassa, hänen on ensin hyvä tietää kaikki parhaat artistit. Yllä mainittu musiikkilehti on julkaissut joka vuoden parhaat (100) laulut vuodesta 1946 tähän vuoteen asti. Näistä listoista löytyvät parhaat artistit.

Kun tietää parhaat artistit, voi etsiä heidän parhaat piisinsä kuuntelemalla bändin kaikki albumit tai vain parhaat hitit.

Internetissä on videoita ja tietoja kaikilta merkittäviltä bändeiltä. Olenkin tutkinut yli tuhannen bändin tuotantoa. Tässä kirjassa on esillä noin 550 artistia. Tämän kirjan kaltainen kirja on ollut mahdollinen vasta sen ajan, kun Internet on ollut olemassa ja siinä on ollut suuri määrä musiikkivideoita. Siis esim. 60- ja 70-luvuilla ei tällaisen kirjan tekeminen olisi ollut helppoa.

MATTI RANTA
20.04.2016

JOHDANTO

Miten löytyvät populaarimusiikin parhaat bändit ja piisit? Ensin tein pitkän listan huomattavan hyvistä artisteista Internetin ja Billboard lehden tietojen avulla. Sitten tutkin näiden artistien parhaat hitit, joiltakin jopa kaikki albumit. Näin saa bändit ja piisit laitettua paremmuusjärjestykseen.

Olen aikaisemmin kirjoittanut englanninkielisen 311 sivuisen kirjan vuonna 2014 - "The best popular music artists and the best pieces of popular music after World War II till 2014, 1200 artists and 8500 songs"(ISBN 978-952-933933-4) - joka on perusteellinen käsikirja. Sitä vastoin tämä käsissä oleva uusi kirja on lyhyt ja hyödyllinen sille, joka haluaa tietää vain kaikista parhaimmat piisit. Parhaimmat bändit ja piisit eivät erotu yhtä hyvin aikaisemmasta kirjasta.

Suuri USA on selvästi tuotteliain musiikkimaa. Heillä on enemmän huippuartisteja ja enemmän tehtyjä piisejä kuin esim. Englannilla, Kanadalla, Irlannilla ja Australialla. Silti näillä kaikilla mailla ovat parhaat bändit ja parhaat piisit tasaväkisiä.

Kun laskee USA:n ja Englannin viidenkymmenen parhaan artistin joukossa olevien naisartistien määrän, huomaa, että USA:lla on viidenkymmenen parhaan artistin joukossa 28 naisvokalistia ja 22 miesvokalistia. Englannilla vastaavat määrät ovat 13 naisartistia ja 37 miesartistia.

Syy on se, että USA:ssa ovat naiskantrimuusikot suurimääräisesti kärjessä, kun taas Englannissa ei harrasteta paljon kantria lähellä olevaa musiikkia. Naiskantrin vallitsevuus USA:ssa siirtää USA:n musiikkityylin poispäin puhtaammasta kitarabändimusiikista viihdemusiikin ja iskelmämusiikin suuntaan. Voi arvata, että se musiikki menestyisi myös Euroviisuissa. Se todennäköisesti kelpaa kansalle helposti niissä maissa, joissa ei harrasteta paljon rokahtavaa kitaramusiikkia.

Paitsi että eniten piisejä tehtailevan USA:n osalta on arvioitu, mitkä ovat 50 parasta bändiä kahden kappaleen perusteella, on heille tehty vielä lista 150 muusta erittäin hyvästä bändistä. Nämä 150 bändiä ovat esillä kirjassa ja lukija voi löytää niiden kaksi tai viisi parasta kappaletta.

Kun esittää listan 50:stä parhaasta bändistä, se on tietysti ainakin jossain määrin subjektiivinen. Kuitenkin lista on hyödyllinen, koska näin noputuu hyvään musiikkiin tutustuminen. Jos jokainen piisi kestää keskimäärin kolme minuuttia, uppoaa 50:n artistin kahden piisin, yhteensä sadan piisin kuunteluun aikaa 300 minuuttia eli viisi tuntia. Se pitkä aika, jonka bändeihin tutustuminen ottaa, oikeuttaa erottelemaan parhaat piisit ja bändit muista.

Mitä tulee Englannin 50:n parhaan bändin listaan, se lienee melko objektiivinen, koska Englannilla ei liene ollut toisen maailmansodan jälkeen paljon enemmän kuin 50 aivan superbändiä. Silti USA:n ja Englannin 50 parasta bändiä lienevät hyvin tasaväkisiä. Pienemmillä musiikkimailla kuin nämä kaksi ei löydy 50 aivan superbändiä.

Kirjassa esitellään USA:n, Englannin ja "muut maat" viidenkymmenen bändin lisäksi yhteensä noin 450 erinomaista yhtyettä ja niiltä viisi tai kaksi huippupiisiä. Käsitys populaarimusiikin sisällöstä tulee täydellisemmäksi, kun esillä on myös Bob Dylanin musiikki. Populaarimusiikin todellisia helmiä ovat monien kuuluisien artistien tulkinnat Dylanin piiseistä. Kirjaan on valittu 80 Dylanin kappaletta. Jokaisesta on 1-10 tulkintaa ja tulkintoja esittäviä artisteja on 130.

50 PARASTA AMERIKKALAISTA ARTISTIA JA HEIDÄN KAKSI HUIPPUPIISIÄÄN

1 AEROSMITH
Crazy
Full circle

2 THE BAND PERRY
Postcard from Paris
Don't let me be lonely

3 THE BANGLES
Where were you when I needed you
Anna Lee

4 MARY J. BLIGE
One
Hard times don't come again no more

5 THE BYRDS
I'll feel a whole lot better
Satisfied mind

6 J.J. CALE
Cocaine
My baby and me

7 KELLY CLARKSON
Breakaway
My life would suck without you

8 RITA COOLIDGE
Loving her was easier
Higher and higher

9 SHERYL CROW
Long road home
C'mon c'mon

10 DIXIE CHICKS
Voice inside my head
Goodbye Earl

11 BOB DYLAN
Just like Tom Thumb's blues
Every grain of sand

12 EAGLES
Take it easy
Tequila sunrise

13 THE EVERLY BROTHERS
Barbara Allen
Lightning express

14 JOHN FOGERTY (CCR)
De ja vu all over again
Centerfield

15 MACY GRAY
Beauty in the world
Love is gonna get ya

16 GUNS AND ROSES
Sweet child of mine
Breakdown

17 EMMILOU HARRIS
Across the border
Goodbye

18 HEART
Who will you run to
All I wanna do is make love to you

19 JOAN JETT
I hate myself for loving you
New Orleans

20 JEWEL
Everybody needs somebody sometime
Sweet home Alabama

21 BON JOVI
Who says you can't go home
Every beat of my heart

22 KRIS KRISTOFFERSON
Loving her was easier
They killed him

23 MIRANDA LAMBERT
Me and Charlie talking
Time to get a gun

24 MARTHA & THE VANDELLAS
Dancing in the street
Jimmy Mack

25 BARRY MCGUIRE
Eve of destruction
Upon a painted ocean

26 SCOTT MCKENZIE
San Francisco
Like an old time movie

27 MELANIE
Carolina in my mind
A hard rain's gonna fall

28 JOHN MELLENCAMP
Pink houses
Teardrops will fall

29 JUICE NEWTON
Angel of the morning
Queen of hearts

30 ROY ORBISON
She's a mystery to me
You got it

31 PETER PAUL AND MARY
Finlandia
Gilgarra mountain

32 TOM PETTY
American girl
Walls

33 WILSON PHILLIPS
Already gone
Don't take me down

34 LADY GAGA
Born this way
Edge of glory

35 POINTER SISTERS
Fire
Fairytale

36 POISON
Every rose has its thorn
I won't forget you

37 SUZI QUATRO
Don't change my luck
I bitt off more than I could chew

38 BONNIE RAITT
Shake a little for me baby
Something to talk about

39 OTIS REDDING
Look at that girl
You left the water running

40 LEANN RIMES
Nothing bout love makes sense
Wasted days & wasted nights

41 LINDA RONSTADT
It's so easy
Silver threads and golden needles

42 JENNIFER RUSH
Twentyfive lovers
Come give me your hand

43 SIMON AND GARFUNKEL
Mrs. Robinson
Graceland

44 BRUCE SPRINGSTEEN
Leap of faith
Brilliant disguise

45 STRAY CATS
Rock this town
Bring it back

46 TAJ MAHAL
She caught the katy
Ez rider

47 CARRIE UNDERWOOD
All American girl
The more boys I meet

48 TLC
Waterfalls
Damaged

49 LEE ANN WOMACK
You've gotta talk to me
Ashes by now

50 ZZ TOP
Gimme all your loving
Bang, bang

LISTA 150:STÄ AMERIKKALAISESTA ARTISTISTA EDELLÄ MAINITTUJEN VIIDENKYMMENEN PARHAAN ARTISTIN LISÄKSI

Koska USA on selvästi tuotteliain maa populaarimusiikin alueella ja sillä on enemmän korkealuokkaisia artisteja kuin muilla mailla, luetellaan alla vielä 150 USAlaista erinomaista muusikkoa. Edellä oli lueteltu 50 muusikkoa niin, että nimen jälkeen oli kaksi erinomaista piisiä. Nyt on siis listassa vain artistien nimet. Itse kukin voi kuitenkin tästä samasta kirjasta löytää kaikki listassa olevat bändit ja heiltä viisi tai kaksi piisiä.

1 Paula Abdul
2 Christina Aguirela
3 Marc Anthony
4 The Archies
5 B-52's
6 Joan Baez
7 Beach Boys
8 Harry Belafonte
9 Brook Benton
10 Chuck Berry
11 Beyonce
12 Big Brother and the Holding Company (Janis Joplin)
13 Blondie
14 The Browns
15 Buckcherry
16 Buffalo Springfield
17 Captain & Tennille
18 Maria Carey
19 Vanessa Carlton
20 Carpenters
21 The Cascades
22 Johnny Cash
23 Tracy Chapman

24 Chubby Checker
25 The Chiffons
26 The Chordettes
27 The Chrystals
28 Rosemary Clooney
29 Coasters
30 Sam Cooke
31 Dee Dee Sharp
32 John Denver
33 Neil Diamond
34 Doors
35 Drifters
36 Melissa Etheridge
37 Betty Everett
38 Everlast
39 Exile
40 Fastball
41 Fergie
42 Roberta Flack
43 Flo Rida
44 Aretha Franklin
45 Glen Frey
46 Gloria Gaynor
47 Bobbi Gentry
48 The Go-Go's
49 Bobby Golsboro
50 Grand Funk Rail-road
51 Green Day
52 Woody Guthrie
53 Jimi Hendrix
54 The Highwaymen
55 Lauryn Hill
56 Keri Hilson
57 Buddy Holly
58 The Honey Cone

59 Johnny Horton
60 Whitney Houston
61 Alan Jackson
62 Mahalia Jackson
63 Michael Jackson
64 Etta James
65 Joni James
66 Jefferson Airplane
67 Kelis
68 The Killers
69 Carole King
70 The Knack
71 Buddy Knox
72 Lenny Kravitz
73 Lady Gaga
74 Little Eva
75 Lloyd
76 Jennifer Lopez
77 Los Lonely Boys
78 Loving Spoonful
79 Madonna
80 Matchbox Twenty
81 Don McLean
82 Natalie Merchant
83 Nicki Minaj
84 Monkees
85 Ella Mae Morse
86 Jason Mraz
87 Nelly
88 Ricky Nelson
89 Neon Trees
90 Tony Orlando
91 Patti Page
92 Dolly Parton
93 Freda Payne

94 Katy Perry
95 Wilson Pickett
96 Pink
97 Elvis Presley
98 Prince
99 Gary Puckett
100 The Pussycat Dolls
101 Eddie Rabbit
102 Rascal Flatts
103 Jerry Reed
104 Red Hot Chili Peppers
105 REM
106 Paul Revere
107 Jimmie Rodgers
108 Diana Ross
109 Barry Sadler
110 Sam the Sham
111 Santana
112 Neil Sedaka
113 Pete Seeger
114 The Shangri-Las
115 The Shirelles
116 Joe Simon
117 Nina Simon
118 Skeeter Davis
119 Snoopdogg
120 Sonny & Cher
121 Britney Spears
122 Kay Starr
123 Jon and Sondra Steele
124 Gwen Stefani (No Doupt)
125 Steve Miller Band
126 Barbra Streisand
127 Sugar Ray
128 Sugarland

129 Donna Summer
130 Taylor Swift
131 Toya
132 Justin Timberlake
133 John Travolta
134 Travis Tritt
135 Tina Turner
136 The Turtles
137 Jimmy Wakely
138 Bobby Vinton
139 Walker Brothers
140 Dionne Warwick
141 We Five
142 Kanye West
143 Margaret Whiting
144 Frank Wilson
145 Gretchen Wilson
146 Amy Winehouse
147 Stevie Wonder
148 The Young Rascals
149 Zac Brown Band
150 The 5th Dimension

50 PARASTA ENGLANTILAISTA ARTISTIA AAKKOSJÄR-JESTYKSESSÄ JA HEIDÄN KAKSI HUIPPUPIISIÄÄN

1 THE ANIMALS (AND ERIC BURDON)
You are on my mind
Sky pilot

2 THE BEATLES
I'm looking through you
Revolution

3 DAVID BOWIE
Rebel rebel
The jean genie

4 PETULA CLARK
Sailor
Downtown

5 CREAM
Sunshine of your love
Outside woman blues

6 DIRE STRAITS (MARK KNOPFLER)
If I had you
Tunnel of love

7 DONOVAN
Rambling boy
Catch the wind

8 DUFFY
Distant dreamer
Put it in perspective

9 EURYTHMICS
The last time
I need a man

10 BRIAN FERRY
Let's stick together
If not for you

11 FINE YOUNG CANNIBALS
Suspicious mind
Blue

12 GEORG HARRISON
Here comes the sun
Bangla Desh

13 HERMAN'S HERMITS
Show me girl
Traveling light

14 THE HOLLIES
Don't let me down
When the ship comes in

15 BILLY IDOL
Sweet sixteen
L.A. woman

16 ELTON JOHN
Skyline pigeon
Sad songs

17 KATRINA & THE WAVES
Going down to Liverpool
The game of love

18 KINKS
Days
Living on a thin line

19 LA ROUX
Colourles colour
Armour love

20 LED ZEPPELIN
Whole lotta love
Black dog

21 JOHN LENNON
Imagine
Happy Christmas

22 LULU
Shout
Feeling alright

23 MANFRED MANN
Pretty flamingo
With God on our side

24 PAUL MCCARTNEY
Mull of Kintyre
No more lonely nights

25 AMY MCDONALD
Spark
Pride

26 GEORG MICHAEL (WHAM)
Wake me up before you go go
Faith

27 MIDDLE OF THE ROAD
Sacramento
Soley soley

28 PAPER LACE
Billy don't be a hero
The night Chicago died

29 PRETENDERS
Thumbelina
Brass in pocket

30 PROCOL HARUM
A whiter shade of pale
Homburg

31 QUEEN
These are the days of our lives
Radio Gaga

32 THE ROLLING STONES
Out of time
Satisfaction

33 S CLUB 7
Some day, some way
Bring the house down

34 SEAL
Like a rolling stone
Manic depression

35 THE SEARCHERS
What have they done to the rain
When you walk in the room

36 SHAKING STEVENS
Marie, Marie
Give me your heart tonight

37 THE SMALL FACES
Itchycoo park
My mind's eye

38 SPENCER DAVIS GROUP
Keep on running
Somebody help me

39 RINGO STARR
Weight of the world
You're sixteen

40 CAT STEVENS
The first cut is the deepest
Morning has broken

41 ROD STEWART
Mandolin wind
Street fighting man

42 STING (POLICE)
Fields of gold
Every breath you take

43 SWEET
Fox on the run
Peppermint twist

44 TANITA TIKARAM
World outside your window
You make the whole world cry

45 THE TREMELOES
My little lady
Twist and shout

46 K.T. TUNSTALL
Hollywood Hill
Let's stick together

47 BONNIE TYLER
Human touch
It's a heartache

48 VAN MORRISON
Browneyed girl
Old black Joe

49 THE WHO
My generation
Let's see action

50 THE YARDBIRDS
Boom boom
Smokestack lightning

50 PARASTA MUUT MAAT -RYHMÄN ARTISTIA AAKKOS-JÄRJESTYKSESSÄ JA HEIDÄN KAKSI HUIPPUBIISIÄÄN

1 A-HA, NORJA
Forever not yours
Crying in the rain

2 ABBA, RUOTSI
Chiquitita
S.O.S.

3 PAUL ANKA, KANADA
Lonely boy
Sealed with a kiss

4 BEE GEES, AUSTRALIA
To love somebody
In the morning

5 LEONARD COHEN, KANADA
So long Marianne
The faith

6 DEBORAH COX, KANADA
Beautiful you are
Baby, you've got what it takes

7 CELINE DION, KANADA
I'm alive
Zora Sourit

8 ENYA, IRLANTI
Long long journey
Pilgrim

9 NELLY FURTADO, KANADA
All good things
Promiscuous girl

10 GALE GARNETT, UUSI-SEELANTI JA KANADA
Pretty boy
We'll sing in the sunshine

11 THE GUESS WHO, KANADA
Shaking all over
American woman

12 DAVID GUETTA, RANSKA
Delirious
I can only imagine

13 ENRIQUE IGLESIAS, ESPANJA
Wish you were here
Bailando

14 INNER CIRCLE, JAMAIKA
Boardwalk
Games people play

15 TERRY JACKS, KANADA
Seasons in the sun
Rock 'n' roll

16 ANTON KARAS, ITÄVALTA
The cafe Mozart waltz
Alt wiener Tanz in c minor

17 ANDY KIM, KANADA
I hear you say
Foundation of my soul

18 LITTLE RIVER BAND, AUSTRALIA
So many paths
Lady

19 GUY LOMBARDO, KANADA
Auld lang syne
Adeste fideles

20 KEVIN LYTTLE, GRENADA
She drives me crazy
Sign your name

21 BOB MARLEY, JAMAIKA
I shot the sheriff
One love

22 PAUL MAURIAT, RANSKA
Je taime
Mamy blue

23 KYLIE MINOGUE, AUSTRALIA
All the lovers
Locomotion

24 SAMATHA MUMBA, IRLANTI
What's it gonna be
Lately

25 ANNE MURRAY, KANADA
Last thing on my mind
Lover's knot

26 YOUSSOU N'DOUR, SENEGAL
Chimes of freedom
Jealous guy

27 NICKELBACK, KANADA
When we stand together
Shaking hands

28 GILBERT O'SULLIVAN, IRLANTI
Nothing rhymed
I'm a writer, not a fighter

29 ORIANTHI, AUSTRALIA
Heaven in this hell
Addicted to love

30 ESTEBAN PAEZ,
My back pages
Romance in Durango

31 THE PEBBLES, BELGIA
Seven horses
I'm sitting by the window

32 PUSSYCAT, HOLLANTI
Mississippi
Rain

33 HELEN REDDY, AUSTRALIA
Delta dawn
I don't know how to love him

34 RIHANNA, BARBAROS
We all want love
Shut up and drive

35 ROXETTE, RUOTSI
How do you do
The look

36 SABRINA, ITALIA
Hot girl
My chico

37 BUFFY SAINTE-MARIE, KANADA
Piney wood hills
Too much is never enough

38 JACK SCOTT, KANADA
When the saints go marching in
You can bet your bottom dollar

39 SEEKERS, AUSTRALIA
The carnival is over
Morningtown ride

40 ERICK SHAGGY, JAMAIKA
Oh Carolina
Piece of my heart

41 SHAKIRA, KOLUMBIA
Waka waka
Se quire, se mata

42 STEPPEN WOLF, KANADA
Born to be wild
Desperation

43 THALIA, MEKSIKO
Con este amor
Insensible

44 SHANIA TWAIN, KANADA
Crime of the century
You shook me all night long

45 U2, IRLANTI
Angel of Harlem
One

46 KEITH URBAN, UUSI-SEELANTI
I never work on Sunday
The river

47 CATERINA VALENTE, ITALIA
Itsy bitsy teenie weenie Honolulu strand bikini
San Francisco

48 MILLI VANILLI, SAKSA
Girl I'm gonna miss you
Baby don't forget my number

49 WEST LIFE, IRLANLTI
I have a dream
The rose

50 NEIL YOUNG, KANADA
Flags of freedom
Downtown

BOB DYLANIN 80 ERINOMAISTA PIISIÄ 130:N ARTISTIN ESITTÄMÄNÄ

Tässä kohdassa on lista Dylanin 80:stä valikoidusta piisistä aakkosjärjestyksessä ja jokaisen piisin yhteydessä on lueteltu yhdestä kymmeneen artistia, jotka ovat tehneet hienon tulkinnan kyseisestä kappaleesta.

Paitsi että Bob Dylan on yksi populaarimusiikin tärkeimmistä säveltäjistä ja tekstintekijöistä, hän on lauluntekijä, jota muut artistit ovat tulkinneet kaikista eniten. Tämä lisää entisestään Bob Dylanin arvoa.

Tässä lyhyessä kirjassa on siis esitelty USA:n, Englannin ja muut maat -ryhmän 50 parasta bändiä. Toiseksi kirjassa on esitelty kahdella tai viidellä kappaleella noin 450 artistia. Hyvä lisä populaarimusiikin kokonaiskuvaan saadaan, kun myös otetaan esiin Dylanin 80 erinomaista piisiä, jotka 130 artista ovat tulkinneet taidokkaasti.

On henkilöitä, jotka eivät kuuntele mielellään Dylanin kaikkia omia esityksiä, mutta kyllä pitävät arvossa eri artistien versioita hänen kappaleistaan. Tämä johtunee suurimmaksi osaksi siitä, että Dylanin konserttiesitykset ovat kovin erilaiset kuin albumeilla olevat studiotaltioinnit. Olen merkinnyt tähdellä ne kappaleet, joissa Dylanin ääni on hyvin edukseen.

1 Absolutely sweet Marie *
Jason and the Schorchers

2 All along the watchtower
Jimi Hendrix
Taj Mahal
Jess Greenberg

3 All I really want to do
Cher

4 As I went out one morning
Mira Billotte

5 The ballad of Frankie Lee and Judas Priest
Yellowman

6 Ballad of a thin man
Stephen Malkmus & The Million Dollar Bashers
The Grass Roots

7 Billy 7
Jim Keltner

8 Black diamond bay
Esteban Paez

9 Blowing in the wind *
Peter Paul and Mary
The Hollies
Bruce Springsteen
Marlene Dietrich
Johnny Cash
Sam Cooke
Janis Joplin
Joan Baez
Cher

10 Can you please crawl out your window?
Jimi Hendrix
Wilko Johnson

11 Chimes of freedom
Bruce Springsteen
Yossou N'Dour
Byrds

12 Desolation row *
Robyn Hitchcock
Fabricio De Andre

13 Don't think twice, it's all right
Indigo Girls

14 Every grain of sand *
Emmilou Harris
Barb Jungr
U2
Lucy Kaplansky
Wolfgang Ambros

15 Farewell Angelina
Joan Baez

16 Forever young
Esteban Paez
Harry Belafonte
Pretenders
Pete Seeger
Wolfgang Ambros (Fur immer jung)

17 Girl from the north country
Hugues Aufray
Francis Cablel
Sam Bush

18 Gotta serve somebody
Erick Burdon
Etta James

19 A hard rain is a'gonna fall
Melanie (Safka)
Joan Baez
U2
The Staple Singers

20 Heart of mine
Norah Jones
Maria Muldaur
Blake Mills

21 Highway 61 revisited
Johnny Winter

22 I believe in you
Allison Krauss
Cat Power

23 I dreamed I saw St. Augustine *
Joan Baez
Dirty Projectors

24 I shall be released
Chrissie Hynde (Pretenders)
Peter Paul and Mary
The Band

25 I threw it all away *
Cher

26 I'll be your baby tonight
Linda Ronstadt
Norah Jones
The Hollies

27 If not for you *
Olivia Newton John
Rod Stewart
George Harrison

28 If you gotta go, go now
Manfred Mann
Cowboy Junkies

29 Inside out
Traveling Wilburys

30 It ain't me babe
Johnny Cash and June Carter
Joan Baez

31 It's all over now baby blue
Van Morrison (Them)
Animals (Eric Burdon)
Byrds
Manfred Mann
Marianne Faitfull
Bonnie Raitt
Joni Mitchell
Bella Wagner
The Chocolate Watchband

32 John Wesley Harding *
J. M. Baule
Mick (Wilkinson)

33 Jokerman
Caetano Veloso

34 Just like a woman *
Manfred Mann
Ricky Nelson
Hollies
Nina Simone
Richie Havens

35 Just like Tom Thumb's blues *
Barry Mcguire
Linda Ronstadt
Neil Young (1993, Tribute to Bob Dylan)
Nina Simone
Robyn Hitchcock

36 Knocking on heaven's door
Avril Lavinge
Erick Clapton
Mark Knopfler
U2
Pink Floyd

37 Lay down your weary tune
Byrds
Jim and Jean
Marley's Ghost
Billy Bragg
Mary Black

38 Lay lady lay
The Everly Brothers
Buddy Guy
Duran Duran
Isaac Hayes
Isley Brothers

39 Leopard-skin pill-box hat
Raphael Saadig
Beck
Peter Parcek

40 License to kill
Cowboy Junkies
Tom Petty
Elvis Costello

41 Like a rolling stone *
Nancy Sinatra
Cher
David Bowie
The Rolling Stones
Green Day
Bon Jovi
Bob Marley
Jimi Hendrix & B.B. King

42 Lily, Rosemary and the Jack of hearts
Mary Lee's Corvette
Joan Baez

43 Love minus zero/ no limit
Eric Clapton
Rod Stewart
Jackson Browne
Ricky Nelson
Walker Brothers
Wolfgang Ambros (Wahre Liebe)

44 Maggie's farm
U2
Hugues Aufray (Maggie La Ferme)

45 Mama you've been on my mind
Rod Stewart
Johnny Cash

46 Man of peace *
Joe Perry

47 Most likely you go your way
Yardbirds

48 Mr. Tambourine man
The Starbugs
Melanie
Byrds
Stevie Wonder

49 My back pages
Esteban Paez
Byrds
Georgia Whiting

50 New morning *
Darren Criss
Maggies Farmers
Grease Band

51 No time to think
Esteban Paez
The Belle Brigade

52 Nothing was delivered
Byrds

53 Oh, sister *
Emmilou Harris
The Black Crowes
Andrew Bird

54 On a night like this
Buckwheat Zydeco
Los Lobos
Rancid

55 One more cup of coffee
The White Stripes
First Aid Kit

56 One of us must know
Mick Hucknall

57 One too many mornings
The Band
The Avett Brothers
Sophie Hunger
Robyn Hitchcock
Mick Hucknall

58 Only a hobo
Rod Stewart

59 Positively 4th street
Jimi Hendrix
Simply Red
Stereophonics
Jerry Garcia

60 Precious angel
Robbie Fulks
Joyce Duo
Bob Dylan's 72nd birthday tribute
Esteban Paez

61 Queen Jane approximately *
Robyn Hitchcock
Grateful Dead
Frank Valli & Four Seasons

62 Romance in Durango
Esteban Paez

63 She belongs to me *
Barry Mcguire
Ricky Nelson

64 Shelter from the storm
Manfred Mann
Andy Hill

65 Slow train coming
Bob Dylan Tribute Band

66 Stuck inside of mobile with the Memphis blues again *
Cat Power
Hugh Cornwell
Grateful Dead

67 Sweetheart like you
Guy Davis

68 Tangled up in blue
The Indigo Girls
K.T. Tunstall
Mary Lee's Corvette

69 Time passes slowly
Judy Collins

70 The times they are a'changing *
Simon & Garfunkel
Peter Paul and Mary
Cher
Phil Collins

71 Tomorrow is a long time *
Rod Stewart
Odetta Holmes
Judy Collins
Elvis Presley
Janet Jones

72 Tonight I'll be staying here with you
Cher
Tina Turner

73 Visions of Johanna
Grateful Dead
Jerry Garcia
Robyn Hitchcock
Marianne Faitfull

74 When I paint my masterpiece
The Band
Elliot Broad

75 When the ship comes in
Peter Paul and Mary
The Hollies

76 With God on our side *
Manfred Mann
Odetta Holmes

77 You angel you
Manfred Mann
Byrds
Maria Muldaur
The Alpha Band

78 You are a big girl now
Mary Lee's Corvette

79 You're gonna make me lonesome when you go
Shawn Colvin

80 You're no good
Jesse Fuller

POPULAARIMUSIIKIN 456 PARASTA BÄNDIÄ

Viiden piisin bändit aakkosjärjestyksessä. Kotimaa ja uran aloittamisvuosi on merkitty ja parhailla artisteilla *-leima. 124 parasta bändiä.

Abba, Ruotsi, 1972, *
Aerosmith, USA, 1970, *

Joan Baez, USA, 1958, *
The Bangles, USA, 1981, *
The Beatles, Englanti, 1960, *
The Beau Brummels, USA, 1964, *
Bee Gees, Australia ja Englanti, 1958, *
Chuck Berry, USA, 1953, *
David Bowie, Englanti, 1962, *
The Browns, USA, 1955, *
Eric Burdon and The Animals, Englanti, 1963, *
The Byrds, USA, 1964, *

JJ Cale, USA, 1958, *
Vanessa Carlton, USA, 1998
Carpenters, USA, 1969
Tracy Chapman, USA, 1986
Leonard Cohen, Kanada, 1956, *
Sheryl Crow, USA, 1985, *
The Crystals, USA, 1960

Dire Straits (Mark Knopfler), Englanti, 1977, *
Dixie Chicks, USA, 1989, *
Donovan, Englanti, 1964, *
Joe Dowell, USA, 1961
Bob Dylan, USA, 1959, *

Eagles, USA, 1971, *
Eurythmics, Englanti, 1980, *
Betty Everett, USA, 1957
The Everly Brothers.USA, 1957, *

Freddy Fender, USA, 1957
Brian Ferry, Englanti, 1970
John Fogerty (CCR), USA, 1959, *

Gale Garnett, Uusi-Seelanti ja Kanada, n.1960, *
The Go-Go's, USA, 1978
Macy Gray, USA, 1988, *

Heart, USA ja Kanada, 1973
Jimi Hendrix, USA, 1963, *
Herman's Hermits, Englanti, 1962, *
The Hollies, Englanti, 1962, *
Buddy Holly, USA, 1949
The Honey Cone, USA, 1969
Johnny Horton, USA, 1950, *

Enrique Iglesias, Espanja, 1995
Inner Circle, Jamaika, 1968

Alan Jackson, USA, 1983
Joan Jett, USA, 1975, *
Jewel, USA, 1994, *
Elton John, Englanti, 1964, *
Marv Johnson, USA, 1956

Katrina & Waves, Englanti, 1981, *
The Killers, USA, 2001, *
Andy Kim, Kanada, 1963
Kinks, Englanti, 1963, *
Lenny Kravitz, USA, 1988, *

Lady Gaga, USA, 2001, *
Frankie Laine, USA, 1937
Miranda Lambert, USA, 2001, *

Manfred Mann, Englanti, 1962, *
Amy Mcdonald, Englanti, 2007, *
Barry Mcguire, USA, n.1962
Melanie, USA, 1967, *
Jo Dee Messina, USA, 1996
Middle Of The Road, Englanti, 1967, *
Ella Mae Morse, USA, 1940
Anne Murray, Kanada, 1968, *

Ricky Nelson, USA, 1949
Juice Newton, USA, 1975
Nickelback, Kanada, 1995

Roy Orbison, USA, 1953, *
Orianthi, Australia, 1997

Esteban Paez,
Pearl Jam, USA, 1990
Peter & Gordon, USA, 1960
Peter, Paul and Mary, USA, 1961, *
Tom Petty, USA, 1969, *
Wilson Phillips, USA, 1989
Wilson Pickett, USA, 1955
Pointer Sisters, USA, 1969, *
Elvis Presley, USA, 1953
Pretenders, Englanti, 1978, *
Pussycat, Hollanti, 1975, *
The Pussycat Dolls, USA, 2003

Eddie Rabbitt, USA, 1964, *
Otis Redding, USA, 1953, *
Cliff Richard, Englanti, 1958
Rihanna, Barbaros, 2005, *
Johnny Rivers, USA, 1956
Tommy Roe, USA, 1959
Kenny Rogers, USA, 1958, *
The Rolling Stones, Englanti, 1962, *
Linda Ronstadt, USA, 1967, *

Buffy Sainte-Marie, Kanada, 1963, *
The Searchers, Englanti, 1959
Pete Seeger, USA, 1939
Seekers, Australia, 1962, *
Shaking Stevens, Englanti, 1968
Dee Dee Sharp, USA, 1961
Simon and Garfunkel, USA, 1957, *
Skeeter Davis, USA, 1952
The Small Faces, Englanti, 1965
Sonny & Cher, USA, 1964, *
Spencer Davis Group, Englanti, 1963
Bruce Springsteen, USA, 1965, *
Gwen Stefani (and No Doupt), USA, 1986
Rod Stewart, Englanti, 1961, *
Sugar Ray, USA, 1986, *
Suzi Quatro, USA, 1964

Taj Mahal, USA, 1964, *
Joe Tex, USA, 1955
Tanita Tikaram, Saksa, USA ja Englanti, 1988, *
TLC, USA, 1990, *
John Travolta, USA, 1969
The Tremeloes, Englanti, 1958
Travis Tritt, USA, 1989
KT Tunstall, Englanti, 2000, *
The Turtles, USA, 1965

U2, Irlanti, 1976, *

Van Morrison (and Them), Englanti, 1958, *
Bobby Vinton, USA, 1959
Walker Brothers, USA, 1964, *
Mary Wells, USA, 1960
The Who, Englanti, 1964, *
Frank Wilson, USA, 1965

Neil Young, Kanada, 1960, *
The Young Rascals, USA, 1965, *

Ne bändit, jotka ovat tässä listassa, voi väittää olevan populäärimusiikin 124 parasta bändiä. Ne bändit, jotka saivat tähti-merkin, voi väittää, että ovat popmusiikin 71 parasta. Mainituista 71:stä bändistä on 40 USA-laisia, 21 englantilaisia, viisi kanadalaisia ja viisi tähteä jakautuvat muille kansakunnille.

Jo nyt otetaan esiin se tilastoaineisto, että 333:sta kahden kappaleen bändistä 80 sai tähtimerkin. 60 tähtimerkkiä sai USA, Englanti 11 ja muille jäi yhteensä yhdeksän tähtileimaa.

VIIDEN MUSIIKKIKAPPALEET LUETTELOT 123:LLE BÄNDILLE.

71 parasta bändiä on saanut *-leiman.

ABBA*
Chiquitita
Nina, pretty ballerina
S.O.S.
Sunny girl
Move on

AEROSMITH *
Eyesight to the blind
All your love
Ain't enough
Full circle
Chip away the stone

THE ANIMALS (AND ERIC BURDON) *
You are on my mind
To love somebody
Sky pilot
The other side of this life
Como Se Llama Mama

JOAN BAEZ *
Battle hymn of the republic
Banks of the Ohio
Farewell, Angelina
Finlandia (A song of peace)
The salt of the earth

THE BANGLES *
Where were you when I needed you
Anna Lee
Going down to Liverpool
September girls
Crash and burn

THE BEATLES *
I'm looking through you
All you need is love
Hey Jude
Revolution
Lady Madonna

THE BEAU BRUMMELS *
You tell me why
You've got to hide your love away
Play with fire
Yesterday
Mr. tambourine man

BEE GEES *
To love somebody
In the morning
Massachusetts
Alone
Don't forget to remember

CHUCK BERRY *
No particular place to go
Memphis Tennessee
Brown eyed handsome man
Roll over Beethoven
Johnny B. Goode

DAVID BOWIE*
Heroes
Rebel rebel
The jean genie
Diamond Dogs
04 starman

THE BROWNS
I heard the bluebirds sing
Send me the pillow
Lonely little Robin
The old country church
They call the wind Maria

THE BYRDS *
See the sky about to rain
Wasn't born to follow
I'll feel a whole lot better
Oh, Susannah
Satisfied mind

J.J. CALE *
Mona
Losers
My baby and me
You got something
Cocaine

VANESSA CARLTON
Carousel
Spring street
Time is on my side
Don't want to be a bride
Happy Christmas

CARPENTERS
Top of the world
Yesterday once more
Please mr. Postman
Jambalaya
Ticket to ride

TRACY CHAPMAN
Bang bang bang
Give me one reason
I used to be a sailor
She's got her ticket
Telling stories

LEONARD COHEN *
So long Marianne
Suzanne
Hey that's no way to say goodbye
Hallelujah
The faith

SHERYL CROW *
Long road home
Members only
C'mon c'mon
Sweet child o'mine
It don't hurt

THE CRYSTALS
Another country, another world
All grown-up
Frankenstein twist
Then he kissed me
Da doo ran ron

DIRE STRAITS (Mark Knopfler) *
If I had you
How long
Ticket to heaven
Tunnel of love
True love will never fade

DIXIE CHICKS *
I believe in love
Goodbye Earl
Voice inside my head
Truth no 2
Everybody knows

DONOVAN *
Catch the wind
Josie
Rambling boy
Colours
Atlantis

JOE DOWELL
Wooden heart
Lilli Marlene
Auf Wiedersehen sweetheart
Oh my papa
Little dolly

BOB DYLAN *
Desolation row (11 minuuttia)
It's all over now baby blue
Positively 4:th street
John Wesley Harding
Every grain of sand

EAGLES *
Peaceful easy feeling
Tequila sunrise
Lying eyes
Hotel California
Take it easy

EURYTHMICS *
I need a Man
The last time
Let's go
Would I lie to you
Missionary man

BETTY EVERETT
The way you do the things
It hurts to be in love
Getting mighty crowded
Hands off
Hound dog

THE EVERLY BROTHERS *
Barbara Allen
Crying in the rain
Take a message to Mary
Lightning express
Always drive cadillac

FREDDY FENDER
Since I met you baby
Before the next teardrop falls
Almost persuaded
Staying in love
Matilda

BRIAN FERRY
The price of love
Let's stick together
Jealous guy
Just like Tom Thumb's blues
If not for you

JOHN FOGERTY (CCR) *
Deja vu all over again
I saw it on tv
Dream song
Southern Streamline
Have you ever seen the rain

GALE GARNETT *
I know you rider
Pretty boy
We'll sing in the sunshine
Prism song
Je n'ai pas si dire non

THE GO-GO S
This old feeling
Apology
We got the beat
Can't stop the world
La la land

MACY GRAY *
Beauty in the world
Kissed it
Love is gonna get ya
Why didn't you call me
She ain't right for you

HEART
Who will you run to
All I wanna do is make love to you
Fanatic
Never
Little queen

JIMI HENDRIX *
Remember
Come on
Purple haze
Hey Joe
Please crawl out your window

HERMAN'S HERMITS *
No milk to day
Show me girl
I'll never dance again
Traveling light
Can't you hear my heartbeat

THE HOLLIES *
He ain't heavy, he is my brother
Stewball
Don't let me down
Blowing in the wind
When the ship comes in

BUDDY HOLLY
Not fade away
Heartbeat
Last kiss
That'll be the day
Oh boy

THE HONEY CONE
One monkey don't stop no show
Sunday morning people
Sitting on a time bomb
Woman can't live by bread alone
All the king's horses

JOHNNY HORTON *
Comanche
The battle of New Orleans
North to Alaska
When it's springtime in Alaska
Honky tonk man

ENRIQUE IGLESIAS
Wish you were here
Ayer
Nunca Te Olvidare
Sad eyes
Bailando

INNER CIRCLE
Boardwalk
Games people play
Black roses
I love girls
Summer jamming

ALAN JACKSON
God bless Texas
If love was a river
Gone country
Buicks to the moon
Chattahoochee

JOAN JETT *
I hate myself for loving you
I love rock n roll
New Orleans
Turn it around
Roadrunner

JEWEL *
Everybody needs somebody sometimes
Proud Mary
Oh! Susanna
Good day
Sweet home Alabama

ELTON JOHN *
Rocket man
Philadelphia freedom
Skyline pigeon
Dixie Lily
Sad songs

MARY JOHNSON
I love the way you love
Move two mountains
I was made to love her
Happy days
I'm not a plaything

KATRINA & THE WAVES *
Walking on sunshine
Love calculator
The game of love
Going down to Liverpool
Love shine a light

KILLERS *
Human
Read my mind
The cowboy's x-mas ball
Neon tiger
Tidal wave

ANDY KIM
Rock me gently
I hear you say
Foundation of my soul
Be my baby
So good together

KINKS *
Death of a clown
Lola
Sunny afternoon
Days
Living on a thin line

LENNY KRAVITZ *
B side blues
American woman
Black and white America
Dig in
Back in Vietnam

LADY GAGA *
Born this way
Edge of glory
Greatest
Hair
G.u.y.

FRANKIE LAINE
High noon
Cool water
Humming bird
Sugarbush
Hanging tree

MIRANDA LAMBERT *
Me and Charlie talking
Time to get a gun
Little red wagon
Old shit
Hard staying sober

MANFRED MANN *
Pretty flamingo
Do wah diddy diddy
Sha la la
It's all over now baby blue
With God on our side

AMY MCDONALD *
Spark
Pride
Love love
Mr. rock n roll
Born to run

BARRY MCGUIRE
Eve of destruction
Just like Tom Thumb's blues
Sins of a family
Upon a painted ocean
Hide your love away

MELANIE (SAFKA) *
What have they done to my song, ma
Carolina in my mind
The good guys
A hard rain's gonna fall
I still haven't found what I'm looking for

JO DEE MESSINA
I'm alright
These are the days
Do you wanna something of it
Burn
Stand by me

MIDDLE OF THE ROAD *
Sacramento
Tweedle dee tweedle dum
Soley soley
Yellow boomerang
Chirpy chirpy cheep cheep

ELLA MAE MORSE
False hearted girl
A little further down the road apiece
A-sleeping at the foot of the bed
Down in Mexico
Get onboard, little children (1942)

ANNE MURRAY *
Last thing on my mind
You won't see me
If you see my saviour
Lover's knot
Both sides now

RICKY NELSON
You are my sunshine
Garden party
Rock n roll lady
Love minus zero/no limit
Lonesome whistle blow

JUICE NEWTON
Angel of the morning
Queen of hearts
Love's been a little bit hard on me
Still the one
A little love

NICKELBACK
When we stand together
Rockstar
Tush
Shaking hands
We will rock you

ROY ORBISON *
California blue
She's a mystery to me
You got it
I drove all night
Distant drums

ORIANTHI
Sunshine of your love
Heaven in this hell
Addicted to love
Fire
Courage

ESTEBAN PAEZ
My back pages
Mr. Tambourine man
No time to think
Romance in Durango
Black diamond bay

PEARL JAM
Supersonic
Come back
You have got to hide your love away
Soldier of love
Last kiss

PETER & GORDON
Five hundred miles
A world without love
Freight train
Exodus song
Pretty Mary

PETER, PAUL AND MARY *
Where have all the flowers gone
Finlandia
Gilgarra mountain
Michael row the boat ashore
Pack up your sorrows

TOM PETTY AND THE HEARTBREAKERS *
Rebels
American girl
Billy the kid
I want back down
Walls

WILSON PHILLIPS
Already gone
A reason to believe
Do it again
Daniel
Go your own way

WILSON PICKETT
Don't fight it
Everybody needs somebody to love
Hey Joe
Land of thousand dances
Mustang Sally

POINTER SISTERS *
Fire
Fairytale
Yes we can can
Turned up too late
Who do you love

ELVIS PRESLEY
Return to sender
Kiss me quick
It's now or never
Tutti frutti
Wooden heart

PRETENDERS *
Middle of the road
Angel of the morning
Thumbelina
Brass in my pocket
I'll stand by you

PUSSYCAT *
Teenage queenie
Mississippi
My broken souvenirs
Daddy
Rain

THE PUSSYCAT DOLLS
Sway
Wait a minute
Buttons
Don't cha
We went as far as felt like going

EDDIE RABBIT *
Drinking my baby off my mind
Driving my life away
Gone too far
She's coming back to say goodbye
On second thought

OTIS REDDING *
Dreams to remember
Hard to handle
Look at the girl
You left the water running
Fa fa fa (Sad song)

BONNIE RAITT, USA, 1971
Love letter
Something to talk about
Shake a little for me baby
Thing called love
Pride and joy

CLIFF RICHARD
The day I met Marie
The young ones
Congratulations
Traveling light
Devil woman

RIHANNA *
Cheers
We all want love
Shut up and drive
Umbrella
Only girl in the world

JOHNNY RIVERS
Mountain of love
Where have all the flowers gone
Positively 4th street
Seventh son
Muddy water

TOMMY ROE
Heart beat
Heather honey
Stagger Lee
Caveman
Crimson and clover

KENNY ROGERS *
Back to the well
Coward of the county
Evening star
Reuben James
Ruby, don't take your love to town

THE ROLLING STONES *

Under the boardwalk
Satisfaction
Under my thumb
Street fighting man
Out of time

LINDA RONSTADT *

It's so easy
Wildflowers
Silver threads and golden needles
Tumbling dice
Love is a rose

BUFFY SAINTE-MARIE *

Piney wood hills
Indian cowboy in the rodeo
Sweet memories
Too much is never enough
Universal soldier

THE SEARCHERS

Needles and pins
What have they done to the rain
When you walk in the room
All my sorrows
Sweets for my sweet

PETE SEEGER

Solidarity for ever
L' Internationale
We shall overcome
What did you learn in school today
Little boxes

THE SEEKERS *
The carnival is over
Morningtown ride
A world of our own
I'll never find another you
I am Australian

SHAKING STEVENS
This ole house
Marie, Marie
Give me your heart tonight
Love attack
I can help

DEE DEE SHARP
I can't stay mad at you
Mashed potato time
Do the bird
We got a thin going on
A woman will do wrong

SIMON AND GARFUNKEL*
Mrs. Robinson
Scarborough fair
Graceland
Mother and child reunion
Duncan

SKEETER DAVIS
My last date
Temporarily out of order
I'm falling too
Blueberry hill
May you never be alone

THE SMALL FACES
You need loving
Sorry she's mine
Itchycoo park
You have really got a hold on me
My mind's eye

SONNY & CHER *
What now my love
I got you baby
The beat goes on
Little man
Wooden heart

SPENCER DAVIS GROUP
Keep on running
Somebody help me
When a man loves a woman
When I come home
Under my thumb

BRUCE SPRINGSTEEN *
Leap of faith
Human touch
Pink cadillac
Brilliant disguise
Girls in their summer clothes

GWEN STEFANI (NO DOUPT)
Rich girl
Hella good
Spider webs
Baby don't lie
Underneath it all

ROD STEWART *
Reason to believe
Mandolin wind
If not for you
Street fighting man
Twisting the night away

SUGAR RAY *
Every morning
Disaster piece
Fly
Someday
Spinning Mary

SUZI QUATRO
Don't change my luck
I bit off more than I could chew
Devil gate drive
Your mama won't like me
Love hurts

TAJ MAHAL *
Good morning mrs. Brown
She caught the Katy
Corrina
Hello Josephine
Ez rider

JOE TEX
A sweet sweet woman
Come in this house
Skinny legs and all
Papa was, too
Sexy sassy wiggle

TANITA TIKARAM *
Good tradition
World outside your window
You make the whole world cry
To wish this
Only the ones we love

TLC *
Waterfalls
Damaged
Red light special
Baby-baby-baby
Unpretty

JOHN TRAVOLTA (AND OLIVIA NEWTON-JOHN)
You're the one that I want
Summer nights
Saturday night fever
Greased lightning
Hopelessly devoted to you

THE TREMELOES
Silence is golden
The lion sleeps today
Yellow river
My little lady
Twist and shout

TRAVIS TRITT
Tougher than the rest
Honky tonk women
Take it easy
She's going home with me
I wish I could go back home

KT TUNSTALL *
Hollywood hill
Let's stick together
My Sharona
Tagled up in blue
Simple twist of faith

THE TURTLES
All my problems
Eve of destruction
Me about you
Bachelor mother
Let me be

U2 *
Angel of Harlem
One
Mysterious ways
A hard rain is a'gonna fall
When love comes to town

VAN MORRISON (AND THEM) *
Brown eyed girl
Hey girl
Old black Joe
It's all over now baby blue
Reminds me of you

BOBBY VINTON
Sealed with a kiss
Halfway to paradise
Over the mountain across the sea
Roses are red
To know you is to love you

WALKER BROTHERS *
Land of 1000 dances
Stand by me
First love never dies
Love minus zero
No regrets

MARY WELLS
What's the matter with you baby
Bye bye baby
Can't you see
The one who really loves you
You beat me to the punch

THE WHO *
My generation
Let's see action
Won't get fooled again
Twist and shout
The last time

FRANK WILSON
He'll learn about her
Last kiss
Tears of happiness
Tell Laura I love her
Young love

NEIL YOUNG *
Flags of freedom
Let's impeach the president
Downtown
Amber Jean
Alabama

THE YOUNG RASCALS *
America the beautiful
Good loving
Grooving
People got to be free
Come on up

KAHDEN MUSIIKKIKAPPALEEN LUETTELOT 333:LLE BÄNDILLE.

80 parasta bändiä on saanut *-merkin. Bändin kotimaa ja uran aloittamisvuosi merkitty.

GREGORY ABBOTT, USA, 1985
Rhyme and reason
Three little birds

PAULA ABDUL, USA, 1978
Ain't never gonna give you up
Alright tonight

CHRISTINA AGUILERA, USA, 1991, *
Candyman
Lady marmalade

A-HA, Norja, 1982
Forever not yours
Crying in the rain

THE ALL-AMERICAN REJECTS, USA, 1999
Walk over me
Heartbeat slowing down

LEROY ANDERSON, USA, n. 1930
Blue tango
Buglers holiday

PAUL ANKA, Kanada, 1955
Lonely boy
Sealed with a kiss

MARC ANTHONY, USA, 1988
Me haces falta
Muy dentro de mi

ARCHIES, USA, 1968
Kissing on sugar sugar
Over and over

LOUIS ARMSTRONG, USA, 1914
When the saints go marching in
We shall overcome

FRANK AVALON, USA, 1951
I'll wait for you
Young love

B-52'S, USA, 1976
Love shack
Private Idaho

THE BAND PERRY, USA, 2005, *
Postcard from Paris
Queen Maybelline

BAY CITY ROLLERS, Englanti, 1966
Rebel rebel
Shang-a-lang

BEACH BOYS, USA, 1961
Barbara Ann
Good vibrations

HARRY BELAFONTE, USA, 1947
Jamaica farewell
Island in the sun

ARCHIE BELL AND THE DRELLS, USA, 1966
Knock on wood
Showdown

TEX BENEKE, USA, n. 1935
When Johnny comes marching home
Chatta nooga choo choo

BROOK BENTON, USA, 1958
Rocking good way
Think twice

BEYONCE, USA, 1997
Videophone
I'd rather go blind

BIG BROTHER & HOLDING COMPANY (AND JANIS JOPLIN), USA, 1965
Call on me
Easy rider

MARY J. BLIGE, USA, 1989, *
One (with U2)
Hard times don't come again no more

BLONDIE, USA, 1974
Heart of glass
The tide is high

BLUE OCTOBER, USA, 1995
Into the ocean
Hate me

DEBBY BOONE, USA, 1971
Are you on the road to loving me again
Perfect fool

BROOKS AND DUNN, USA, 1990
Every river
One more roll of the dice

ANITA BRYANT, USA, 1956
Please help me, I'm falling
A Texan and a girl from Mexico

BUCKCHERRY, USA, 1995, *
Borderline
Pump it up

GLEN CAMPBELL, USA, 1958
All I have to do is dream
It's only make believe

CAPTAIN & TENNILLE, USA, 1974, *
Wedding song
I'm on my way

MARIAH CAREY, USA, 1988
Dreamlover
Touch my body

ERIC CARMEN, USA, 1967
She did it
That's rock n roll

THE CARS, USA, 1976
Let's go
Keep on knocking

THE CASCADES, USA, 1960, *
Rhythm of the falling rain
Dreaming

JOHNNY CASH, USA, 1954
I was there when it happened
One

SHAUN CASSIDY, USA, 1976
Bad boy
Da doo ron ron

CHAMILLIONAIRE, USA, 1997
True
Good morning

CHUBBY CHECKER, USA, 1959, *
Loddy lo
Limbo rock

CHER, USA.1963, *
If I could turn back time
Like a rolling stone

MARK CHESNUT, USA, 1988, *
Full blooded Texan
Ol' country

THE CHIFFONS, USA, 1960
One fine day
My boyfriend's back

THE CHORDETTES, USA, 1946
Never on Sunday
A broken vow

DEE CLARK, USA, 1952
Hey little girl
Just keep it up

PETULA CLARK, Englanti, 1939, *
Downtown
Sailor

KELLY CLARKSON, USA, 2002 *
Breakaway
My life would suck without you

PATSY CLINE, USA, 1947
The heart you break may be your own
I've loved and lost again

ROSEMARY CLOONEY, USA, 1946
Beautiful brown eyes
This ole house

COASTERS, USA, 1955
Little Egypt
Young blood

COBRA STARSHIP, USA, 2005
Good girls go bad
Fool like me

SAM COOKE, USA, 1951
Another Saturday night
Twisting the night away

RITA COOLIDGE, USA, 1969, *
Loving her was easier
The way you do things you do

DEBORAH COX, Kanada, 1995
Beautiful you are
Baby, you've got what it takes

FLOYD CRAMER, USA, n. 1953
Last date
When a man loves a woman

CRAZY TOWN, USA, 1995
Darkside
Battle cry

CREAM, Englanti, 1966
Sunshine of your love
Outside woman blues

MILEY CYRUS, USA, 2001
You and me together
Learned from you

PAUL DAVIS, USA, 1958, *
I just wanna keep it together
Thinking of you

DORIS DAY, USA, 1939
Sugarbush
Everybody loves a lover

TAYLOR DAYNE, USA, 1985
With every beat of my heart
Tell it to my heart

GAVIN DEGRAW, USA, 1990
I don't want to be
Just friends

DEM FRANCHIZE BOYZ, USA, 2004
White tee
Riding rims

JOHN DENVER, USA, 1962 *
Annie's song
Some days are diamonds

NEIL DIAMOND, USA, 1962
Jonathan Livingstone seagull-skybird
Lonely looking sky

DIAMOND RIO, USA.1982
Beautiful mess
In God we still trust

DIDO, Englanti, 1995
Never want to say it's love
White flag

CELINE DION, Kanada, 1980
I'm alive
Zora Sourit

DOORS, USA, 1965
Tight rope ride
The Peking king and the New York queen

CAROL DOUGLAS, USA, n. 1974
Light my fire
Burning

DR. DRE, USA, 1984
Xx plosive
Housewife

DR. HOOK, USA, 1967
When you are in love with a beautiful woman
Only sixteen

DRIFTERS, USA, 1953
Under the boardwalk
Save the last dance for me

DUFFY, Englanti, 2004, *
Distant dreamer
Put it in perspective

D12, USA, 1996
How come
My band

ELLIOT MISSY, USA, 1991
Shake your pom pom
Gossip folks

EMINEM, USA, 1989*
Shake that ass for me
Guts over fear

EN VOGUE, USA, 1989
Free your mind
Those dogs

ENYA, Irlanti, 1980
Pilgrim
Long long journey

ESTELLE, Englanti, 2004
Go gone
No substitute love

MELISSA ETHERIDGE, USA, 1985, *
Lucky
If I only wanted to

EVE, USA, 1998
Set it on fire
Let me blow ya mind

EVERLAST, USA, 1989
Seven years
One and the same

EXILE, USA, 1978
She's a miracle
Kiss you all over

FAITH EVANS, USA, 1994
Dumb
I'll be missing you

FAITH HILL USA, 1993
Piece of my heart
Little drummer boy

FASTBALL, USA, 1995
Better than it was
You're an ocean

FERGIE (BLACK EYED PEAS), USA, 1984
My humps
Clumsy

FINE YOUNG CANNIBALS, Englanti, 1984
Blue
Suspicious minds

ROBERTA FLACK, USA, 1959, *
We can work it out
Hey, that's no way to say goodbye

FLO RIDA, USA, 2006
Club can't handle me
Rewind

FOO FIGHTERS, USA, 1994
Long road to ruin
Wheels

FOREIGNER, USA, 1976
Hot blooded
I want to know what love is

THE FOUR TOPS, USA, 1953
The last train to Clarksville
If I were a carpenter

CONNIE FRANCIS, USA, 1943
Never on a Sunday
Quizas quizas quizas

ARETHA FRANKLIN, USA, 1956
Pink Cadillac
Mockingbird

GLENN FREY, USA, 1966
Part of me, part of you
Route 66

NELLY FURTADO, Kanada, 1996
All good things
Promiscuous girl

MARVIN GAYE, USA, 1963
Baby don't you do it
Ain't that peculiar

GLORIA GAYNOR, USA, 1965
Honeybee
I never knew

THE J. GEILS BAND, USA, 1967, *
Love stinks
Angel in blue

BOBBIE GENTRY, USA, 1964, *
Ode to Billie Joe
My elusive dreams

GERRY & THE PACEMAKESS, Englanti, 1959
Chills
Jambalaya

GEORGIA GIBBS, USA, 1936
Seven lonely days
Let him know

JIMMY GILMER, USA, n. 1959
Bottle of wine
Go Jimmy go

GLADY'S KNIGHT, USA, 1953
I heard it through grapevine
Every beat of my heart

BOBBY GOLSBORO, USA, 1962
Honey
See the funny little clown

GOO GOO DOLLS, USA, 1986
Sweetest lie
Now I hear

GRAND FUNK RAILROAD, USA, 1969
We're an American band
Time machine

AMY GRANT, USA, 1976
Takes a little time
Big yellow taxi

AL GREEN, USA, 1967
I want to hold your hand
Take me to the river

GREEN DAY, USA, 1986, *
Last of American girls
Like a rolling stone

THE GUESS WHO, Kanada, 1962
Shaking all over
American woman

DAVID GUETTA, Ranska, 1984
Delirious
I can only imagine

GUNS AND ROSES, USA, 1985
Sweet child of mine
Breakdown

WOODY GUTHRIE, USA, 1930
Jesus Christ
1913 massacre

BILL HALEY, USA, 1946
Hail hail rock n roll
God bless rock, 'n' roll

EMMYLOU HARRIS
Across the border
Goodbye

GEORG HARRISON, Englanti, 1958
Here comes the sun
Bangla Desh

WILLBERT HARRISON USA, n. 1950
Kansas city
Forgive me

BILL HAYES, USA, 1952
The yellow rose of Texas
Ballad of Davy Crockett

DON HENLEY, USA, 1970
Dirty laundry
All she wants to do is dance

THE HIGHWAYMEN, USA, 1985
American remains
The city of New Orleans

LAURYN HILL, USA, 1991
Every ghetto, every city
Redemption song

KERI HILSON, USA, 2001, *
Pretty girl rock
Lose control

HINDER, USA, 2001
All American nightmare
2 sides of me

THELMA HOUSTON, USA, 1966
Don't leave me this way
And I thought you loved me

WHITNEY HOUSTON, USA, 1977, *
I wanna dance with somebody
How will I know

BILLY IDOL, Englanti, 1977
Sweet sixteen
L.A. woman

TERRY JACKS, Kanada, 1962, *
Seasons in the sun
Rock n roll

JANET JACKSON, USA, 1973
Two to the power of love
What'll I do

LA TOYA JACKSON, USA, 1972
Heart don't lie
Reggae nights

MAHALIA JACKSON, USA, 1927
He's got the whole world in his hands
Go tell it on the mountain

MICHAEL JACKSON, USA, 1964
Black or white
Beat it

ETTA JAMES
I've got dreams to remember
God's song

JONI JAMES, USA, 1952
Danny boy
Sweet talk

TOMMY JAMES & SHONDELLS, USA, 1959
Sweet cherry wine
Crimson and clover

JEFFERSON AIRPLANE, USA, 1965, *
White rabbit
Angel of the morning

BILLY JOEL, USA, 1965
We didn't start the fire
You may be right

ROBERT JOHN, USA, n. 1958
Stay a little longer
The lion sleeps tonight

TOM JONES, Englanti, 1953
Delilah
Detroit city

JOURNEY, USA, 1973
Lights
Faitfully

BON JOVI, USA, 1983, *
Who says you can't go home
Every beat of my heart

DANITY KANE, USA, 2005, *
Bad girl
One shot

ANTON KARAS, Itävalta, n. 1943
The cafe Mozart Waltz
Alt wiener Tanz in c minor

KELTS, USA, 1997, *
Acapella
Brass in pocket

KID ROCK, USA, 1990
All summer long
Only God knows why

BB KING, USA, 1948
Something you got
We are gonna make it

CAROLE KING, USA, 1958
Will you still love me tomorrow
Child of mine

THE KNACK, USA, 1978, *
Can't put price on love
Corporation shuffle

BUDDY KNOX, USA, 1955, *
Storm clouds
Lovey dovey

BILLY J. KRAMER, Englanti, 1963
Boys cry
I'll be a doggone

KRIS KRISTOFFERSON, USA, 1966, *
Loving her was easier
They killed him

LA ROUX, Englanti, 2006
Colourles colour
Armour love

CYNDI LAUPER, USA, 1980
Time after time
I drove all night

LED ZEPPELIN, Englanti, 1968, *
Whole lotta love
Black dog

JOHN LENNON, Englanti, 1957
Imagine
Happy Christmas

LES BAXTER, USA, n. 1956
Blue tango
Tango of the drums

LES PAUL AND MARY FORD, USA, n. 1950
Meet mister Callaghan
Vaya con dies

GARY LEWIS AND THE PLAYBOYS, USA, 1960
Sealed with a kiss
I saw Elvis Presley last night

HUEY LEWIS & THE NEWS, USA, 1967
Do you believe in love
Buzz buzz buzz

LIPPS INC., USA, 1979
Funky town
All night dancing

LITTLE EVA, USA, 1962 *
The locomotion
Another night with the boys

LITTLE RICHARD, USA, 1947
Tutti frutti
Lucille

LITTLE RIVER BAND, Australia, 1975
So many paths
Lady

LLOYD, USA, 1996
World cry
Dedication to my ex

LLOYD PRICE, USA, 1952
I'm gonna get married
Personality

LMFAO, USA, 2006
Sexy and I know it
Party rock anthem

GUY LOMBARDO, Kanada, 1924
Auld Lang syne
Adeste Fideles

JENNIFER LOPEZ, USA, 1986
Baila
On the floor

LOS LONELY BOYS, USA, 1996, *
Diamonds
Believe

LOVING SPOONFUL, USA, n.1964, *
You and me and rain on the roof
Nashville cats

LULU, Englanti, 1964, *
Shout
Feeling alright

FRANKIE LYMON, USA, 1954
Short fat Fannie
Diana

VERA LYNN, Englanti, 1935
Rose of England
Amazing grace

KEVIN LYTTLE, Grenada, 2001
She drives me crazy
Sign your name

MARY MACGREGOR, USA, 1976, *
Dreary black hills
The wedding song

MADONNA, USA, 1979, *
True blue
Material girl

THE MAMAS & THE PAPAS, USA, 1965
Dancing in the street
Dedicated to the one I love

THE MANHATTANS, USA, 1962
All I need is your love
It's so hard loving you

BOB MARLEY, Jamaika, 1962 *
I shot the sheriff
One love

MARTHA & THE VANDELLAS, USA, 1957, *
Dancing in the streets
Jinmy Mack

AL MARTINO, USA, 1943
What now my love
Come share the wine

MATCHBOX TWENTY, USA, 1995
Come dancing
3 AM

PAUL MAURIAT, Ranska, n. 1950
Je taime
Mamy blue

PAUL MCCARTNEY, Englanti, 1957, *
Mull of Kintyre
No more lonely nights

TIM MCGRAW, USA, 1990
Southern voice
Real good man

THE MCGUIRE SISTERS, USA, 1952
Sugartime
Just for old time's sake

SCOTT MCKENZIE, USA, n. 1955, *
San Francisco
Like an old time movie

DON MCLEAN, USA, 1969
American pie
Everyday

JOHN MELLENCAMP, USA, 1976 *
Pink houses
Teardrops will fall

NATALIE MERCHANT, USA, 1991
Gun shy
Carnival

MIA, Englanti, 2000
Paper planes
Hoffnung

GEORG MICHAEL (WHAM), Englanti, 1981 *
Wake me up before you go go
Faith

NICKI MINAJ, USA, 2004
Pound the alarm
Starships

KYLIE MINOGUE, Australia, 1979, *
All the lovers
Locomotion

MOBY, USA, 1984
Beautiful
South side

MONKEES, USA, 1966
I'm a believer
Daydream believer

MOODY BUES, Englanti, 1964
Melancoly man
Nights in white satin

ART MOONEY, USA, n. 1947
Banjo boy
I never see Maggie alone

ALANIS MORISSETTE, Kanada ja USA, 1985
21 things that I want in a lover
Lens

MOUNTAIN, USA, 1969
Flowers of evil
Dreams of milk and honey

JASON MRAZ, USA, 1999
Spirit in the sky
93 million miles

SHAWN MULLINS, USA, 1990, *
Faith
The ballad of Kathryn Johnston

SAMATHA MULLINS, Irlanti, 1999, *
What's it gonna be
Lately

YOUSSOU N'DOUR, Senegal, 1975 *
Chimes of freedom
Jealous guy

NELLY, USA, 1993
Country grammar
Nothing without her

NEON TREES, USA, 2005
Mad love
Moving in the dark

NEW SEEKERS, Englanti, 1969
I'd like to teach the world to sing
Dance dance dance

OLIVIA NEWTON-JOHN, Australia ja Englanti, 1963
If not for you
Don't cry for me Argentina

GILBERT O'SULLIVAN, Irlanti, 1964
Nothing rhymed
I'm a writer, not a fighter

TONY ORLANDO & DAWN, USA, 1961
If only he would
Halfway to paradise

JAKE OWEN, USA, 2004
Nobody feeling no pain
Yee haw

PATTI PAGE, USA, 1946
Mocking bird hill
How much is that doggie in the window

BRAD PAISLEY, USA, 1999
All you really need is love
Let the good times roll

ROBERT PALMER, Englanti, 1964
Addicted to love
Simply irresistable

PAPER LACE, Englanti, 1967
Billy don't be a hero
The night Chicago died

RAY PARKER JR, USA, n. 1980
The other woman
Dock of the bay

DOLLY PARTON, USA, 1956
Coat of many colours
Letter to heaven

FREDA PAYNE, USA, 1962 *
Bring the boys home
Soul train

THE PEBBLES, Belgia, 1965
Seven horses
I'm sitting by the window

CECE PENISTON, USA, 1991
Moving on
We got a love thang

CARL PERKINS, USA, 1946
Pink pedal pusher
Blue suede shoes

KATY PERRY, USA, 2001
Hot n' cold
Hackensack

PET SHOP BOYS, Englanti, 1981
Always on my mind
Go west

PINK, USA, 1995, *
18 Wheeler
Me and Bobby McGee

PISTOL ANNIES, USA, 2011, *
Taking pills
Hell on heels

PITBULL, USA, 2001
Castle made of sand
Back in time

GENE PITNEY, USA, 1961
Hello Mary Lou
Dedication

THE PLATTERS, USA, 1954
Twilight time
Great pretender

POISON, USA, 1983
Every rose has its thorn
I won't forget you

JOHNNY PRESTON, USA, 1959
I want a rock and roll quitar
City of tears

PRINCE, USA, 1976, *
Raspberry beret
Purple rain

PROCOL HARUM, Englanti, 1967, *
A whiter shade of pale
Homburg

GARY PUCKETT & THE UNION GAP, USA, 1967
Lady Madonna
Don't make promises

QUEEN, Englanti, 1970, *
These are the days of our lives
Radio Gaga

RASCAL FLATTS, USA, 1999
Revolution
Lean on me

RED FOLEY, USA, 1930
One by one
Peace in the valley

RED HOT CHILI PEPPERS, USA, 1983
Dani California
Hey

HELEN REDDY .Australia, 1970, *
Delta dawn
I don't know how to love him

JERRY REED, USA, 1956
Boys of 44
Down on the corner

JIM REEVES, USA, 1948, *
Distant drums
Oklahoma hills

R.E.M., USA, 1980, *
Man on the moon
What's the frequency, Kenneth

PAUL SEVERE & THE RAIDERS, USA, 1958, *
Prince of peace
Ups and downs

LIONEL RICHIE, USA, 1968
Dancing on the ceiling
Say you, say me

RIGHTEOUS BROTHERS, USA, 1962
My babe
You can have her

LEANN RIMES, USA, 1991, *
Nothing bout love makes sense
Wasted days & wasted nights

JIMMIE RODGERS, USA, 1927
Hobo Bill's last ride (1929)
Traveling blues (1931)

DIANA ROSS AND THE SUPREMES, USA, 1959
Baby love
Stop in the name of love

ROXETTE, Ruotsi, 1986
How do you do
The look

JENNIFER RUSH, USA, 1979, *
25 lovers
Come give me your hand

BOBBY RYDELL, USA, 1958
We got love
The cha cha cha

S CLUB 7, Englanti, 1998
Some day, some way
Bring the house down

SABRINA, Italia, n.1987, *
Hot girl
My chico

BARRY SADLER, USA, 1966, *
The ballad of the green berets
Letter from Vietnam

SAM THE SHAM AND THE PHARAOHS, USA, n. 1965
Little Red Riding Hood
Gangster of love

SALT 'N' PEPA, USA, 1985
I am the body beautiful
Whatta man

SANTANA, USA, 1967
Ain't superstitious
Whole lotta love

JACK SCOTT, Kanada, 1957
When the saints go marching in
You can bet your bottom dollar

LINDA SCOTT, USA, n. 1957
I've told every little star
Don't bet money honey

SEAL, Englanti, 1987, *
Like a rolling stone
Manic depression

NEIL SEDAKA, USA, 1957, *
The queen of 1964
I go ape

THE SENSATIONS, n. 1968
I found my love
Those guys

ERICK SHAGGY, Jamaika, 1993, *
Oh Carolina
Piece of my heart

SHAKIRA, Kolumbia, 1990
Waka waka
Se quire, se mata

THE SHANGRI-LAS, USA, 1963
Sophisticated boom boom
The dum dum ditty

DEL SHANNON, USA, 1958
Walk away
Runaway

THE SHIRELLES, USA, 1957, *
Dancing in the street
Voice of experience

CARLY SIMON, USA, 1964
Mockingbird
You're so vain

JOE SIMON, USA, 1959, *
My adorable one
Yours love

NINA SIMON, USA, 1954, *
Gin house blues
Trouble in mind

SIXPENCE, USA, 1992
I can't catch you
There she goes

SNOOP DOGG, USA, 1992
Why did you leave me
Snoop afelia

BRITNEY SPEARS, USA, 1992
We will rock you (Pepsi)
Baby one more time

BUFFALO SPRINGFIELD, USA, 1966
Mr. Soul
Hot dusty roads

JIM STAFFORD, USA, 1974
Don't fool around when there's a fool around
Don't forget the hard times

THE STAPLE SINGERS, USA, 1948
A hard rain is a'gonna fall
People get ready

KAY STARR, USA, 1939
Rock and roll waltz
Side by side

RINGO STARR, Englanti, 1957
Weight of the world
You're sixteen

JON AND SONDRA STEELE,
How much do you love me
My happiness

STEPPENWOLF, Kanada, 1967
Born to be wild
Desperation

STEVE MILLER BAND, USA, 1966
Take the money and run
Mercury blues

CAT STEVENS, Englanti, 1965
The first cut is the deepest
Morning has broken

STING, Englanti, 1971, *
Fields of gold
Every breath you take

STRAY CATS, USA, 1979, *
Rock this town
Rip it up

BARBRA STREISAND, USA, 1955
Memories
Woman in love

THE STRING-A-LONGS, USA, n. 1961
Red river twist
Blue guitar

SUGARS, USA, 2002
It happens
Tennessee

DONNA SUMMER, USA, 1968
On the radio
Rumours has it

SWEET, Englanti, 1958, *
Fox on the run
Peppermint twist

TAYLOR SWIFT, USA, 2004
American girl
Tim Mcgraw

THE TEMPTATIONS, USA, 1960
My girl
A place in the sun

TENNESSEE ERNIE FORD, USA, n. 1940
Ballad of Davy Crockett
The old rugged cross

THALIA, Meksiko, 1981
Con Este Amor
Insensible

THOMPSON SQUARE, USA, 2002
As bad as it gets
Getaway car

TIFFANY, USA, 1981
I saw him standing there
Radio romance

TIMBALAND, USA, 1990
If we ever meet again
Give it to me

JUSTIN TIMBERLAKE, USA, 1992
Work it
4 minutes

TOYA, USA, 2001, *
I do
No matta what

TRAIN, USA, 1994
Hey, soul sister
She's on fire

TRAVELING WILBURYS, USA ja Englanti, 1988, *
Handle with care
Inside out

TINA TURNER, USA, 1958, *
It's gonna work out fine
Philadelphia freedom

SHANIA TWAIN, Kanada, 1993, *
Crime of the century
You shook me all night long

BONNIE TYLER, Englanti, 1975
Human touch
Lost in France

UNCLE CRACKER, USA, 1987, *
Drift away
Letter to my daughter

CARRIE UNDERWOOD, USA, 2005
All American girl
The more boys I meet

KEITH URBAN, Uusi-Seelanti, 1991
I never work on Sunday
The river

URIAH HEEP, Englanti, 1969
Lady in black
Easy living

CATERINA VALENTE, Italia, 1953
Itsy bitsy teenie weenie Honolulu strand bikini
San Francisco

MILLI VANILLI, Saksa, 1988
Girl I'm gonna miss you
Baby don't forget my number

BILLY VAUGHN, USA, n. 1952
Blue hawaii
Raunchy

BOBBY VEE, USA, 1959
More than I can say
Come back when you grow up girl

VILLAGE STOMPERS, USA, n. 1962
Dominique
Midnight in Moscow

ADAM WADE, USA, 1959
Take good care of her
The writing on the wall

JIMMY WAKELY, USA, 1939
Wedding bells
Beautiful brown eyes

WAR (Eric Burden), USA, 1969
Low rider
Outlaw

DIONNE WARWICK, USA, 1962
Trains and boats and planes
Heartbreaker

WE FIVE, USA, 1964, *
I can never go home again
Here comes the sun

KANYE WEST, USA, 1996
Gold digger
Diamonds from Sierra Leone

WEST LIFE, Irlanti, 1998
I have a dream
The rose

MARGARET WHITING, USA, 1942
The wheel of hurt
Foggy river

TEX WILLIAMS, USA, 1946
Senator from Tennessee
I got Texas in my soul

GRETCHEN WILSON, USA, 2004
California girls
Redneck woman

AMY WINEHOUSE, USA, 2003, *
Rehab
Hey little rich girl

BILL WITHERS, USA, 1963
Harlem
Heartbreak road

LEE ANN WOMACK, USA, 1992, *
You've gotta talk to me
Ashes by now

STEVIE WONDER, USA, 1961
A place in the sun
Living for the city

THE YARDBIRDS, Englanti, 1963
Boom boom
Smokestack lightning

YOUNG MONEY, USA, 2005
Play in my band
Every girl

ZAC BROWN BAND, USA, 2002
I play the road
Where the boat leaves from

ZZ TOP, USA, 1969 *
Gimme all your loving
Bang, bang

3LW, USA, 1999
More than friends
High fashion

THE 5TH DIMENSION, USA, 1966
Aquarius/Let the sunshine in
Puppet man

1910 FRUITGUM COMPANY, USA, 1965
No good Annie
Special delivery

? & THE MYSTERIANS, USA, 1962
Ten o'clock
Upside